Christmas 2005

To Deb, my sister of choice and
by choice.

Love,

Jill

D0031856

The Uh-Oh Heart

The Uh-Oh Heart

by Sandy Gingras

Down The Shore Publishing
Harvey Cedars, NJ

Illustrations and text copyright 2003 Sandra A. Gingras. All rights reserved.
Material in this book may not be used or reproduced, in whole or in part, in any form or by any means, electronic or mechanical, including photocopying, video or other recording, or by any information storage or retrieval system, without written permission, except in the case of brief quotations embodied in critical articles and reviews. For information, contact the publisher at the address below.

Down The Shore Publishing Corp.
Box 3100, Harvey Cedars, NJ 08008
www.down-the-shore.com

The words "Down The Shore" and the Down The Shore Publishing logo
are a registered U.S. Trademark.

Printed in China
2 4 6 8 10 9 7 5 3 1
First Printing

Library of Congress Cataloging-in-Publication Data

Gingras, Sandy, 1958-
The uh-oh heart / by Sandy Gingras.
p. cm.
ISBN 0-945582-96-X
1. Love-Miscellanea. I. Title

BF575.L8 G565 2003
177'.7-dc21

for
John Butler
the
anti-bad

Once upon a time

There was an uh-oh heart.
It lived far away and safe-safe,
tired of the chance-chance world.

It wanted only

To be left alone, through its same-same nights and so-so days.

It beaT-beaT iTs drum.

It putt-putted along its careful course.

If another heart offered,
the uh-oh heart said uh-oh.

If a cloud came by, the uh-oh heart

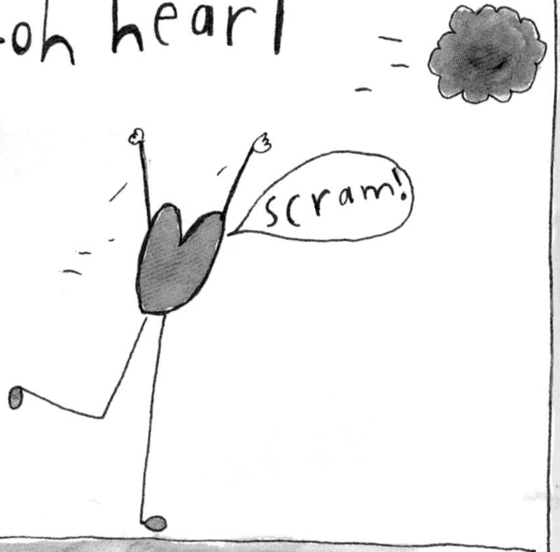

chased it away...

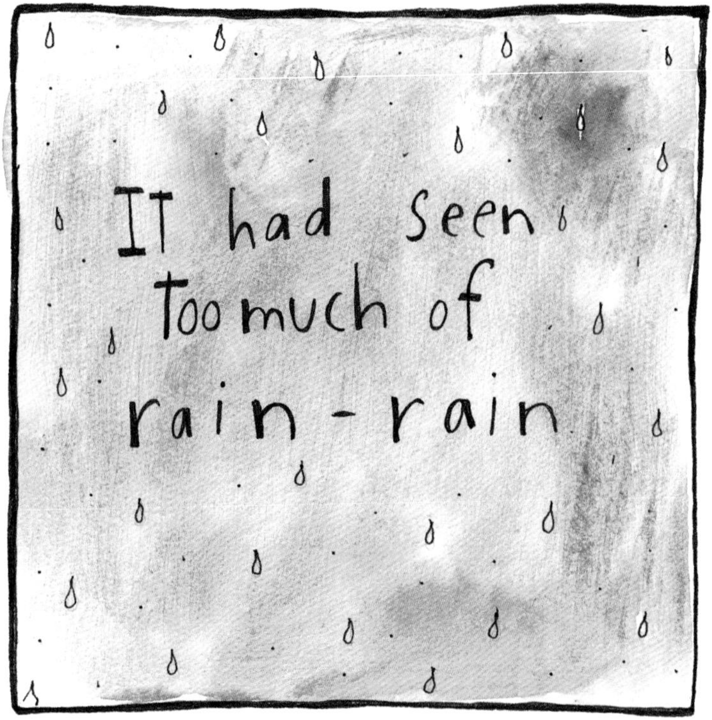
IT had seen
too much of
rain - rain

It kept up a steady

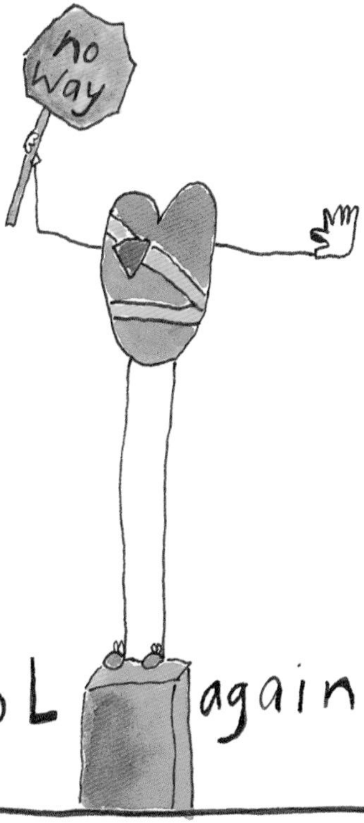

patrol against life-life...

and change-change.

But one night, the moon was so full-full, it spilled into the uh-oh house and pulled the uh-oh heart out of bed. "Why is the world so glow-glow?" the uh-oh heart thought.

But

The moon did not...

The uh-oh heart climbed
up-up. "Stop," the uh-oh heart
told the moon, "Stop."

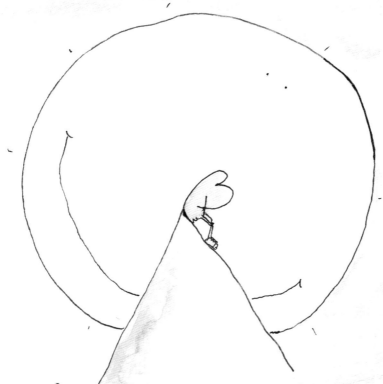

for There are some Things
bigger Than an uh-oh hearT.

The next day,

the sun
rose-rose
as it does

The uh-oh heart woke
To a knock-knock.

It opened up To a
new hearT and the worLd
changed... changed...

The new heart said, "You don't need your uh-ohs anymore. Come away-away with me."

The uh-oh heart was un-unsure,

buT, in THiS worLd,
There are sTronger
Things Than fear-
fear...

"Let go," the new heart said, "trust." It had a clickety-clack way of talking like a train going fast-fast.

The uh-oh heart
feLT in a fog-fog

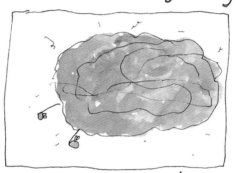

It was spooky
and LosT...
buT ThriLL-ThriLL.

The uh-oh hearT was changing....

and iT was good.

So, it left behind its uh-oh's in a lock-lock drawer
but where... why
flow baby flow
and set off...

It went on wild
flights through
flutter-
flutter
nights
aLL the way up To
The moon.

♪ shoobydoobydoo ♪

It Learned how

To cha - cha...

To Tra-La-La

and

ha-ha

One bright brave day the uh-oh heart felt like a flock of birds swoop-swooped inside of it. It open opened, but it was not birds that came out...

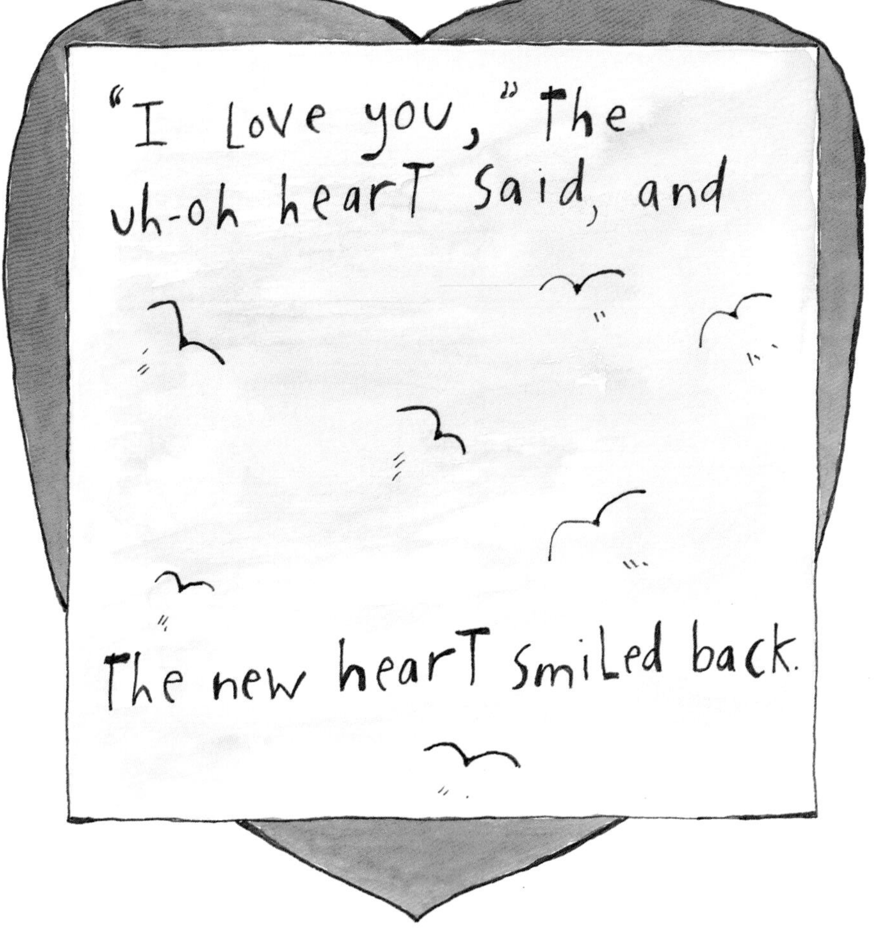

"I love you," the uh-oh heart said, and

the new heart smiled back.

It was
a
shine-
shine
day.

"Uh-oh"

The uh-oh
heart said.

The sky got grey.

The uh-oh heart fell flat. flat.

The uh-oh hearT was blue-bLue.

It could not feel
The sun-sun on its face

or The world wing-winging
it all around.

Time passed

The uh-oh heart could barely stand it.

The world kept on with its stubborn Talk-Talk, live-live ways.

The world kept on with
its sing-sing song...

UnTiL The uh-oh hearT
was sick - sick of iT...

"Stop," the uh-oh heart said, "Stop."

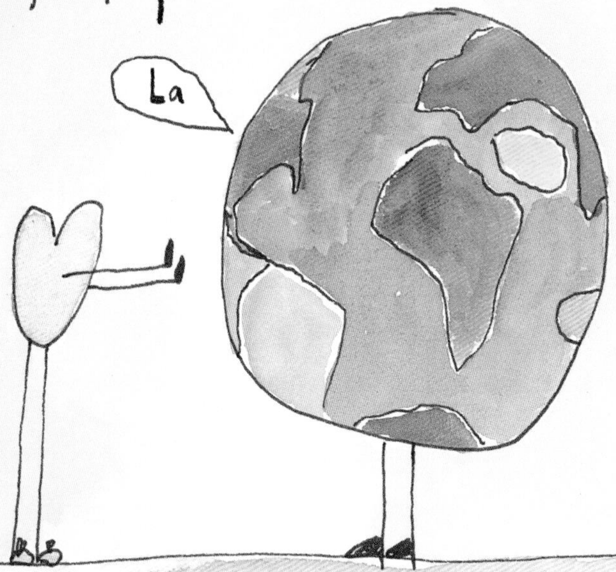

but the world would not.

"Why?" The uh-oh heart
yelled To The sky-sky:
"Why does The moon pull-pull?
Why does love change-change?
Why does The world sing-
Sing... if iT's all for nothing?"
BuT The sky answered noT.

ALThough The uh-oh
hearT could noT hear
iT, The sky was full
of quieT-quieT moving
Things, answers with
their own wings...

So, The uh-oh hearT goT
iTself up on iTs wobble-wobble
Legs and Took one shaky-shake
sTep and Then anoTher

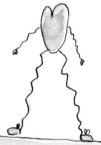

and made iT back To its uh-oh house

and The peacefuL easy-easy of iTs uh-oh worLd where The sun-sun shone and The breezy-breezes bLew.

The uh-oh heart had returned to its uh-oh Life! IT sigh-sighed with relief. It found its old drawer of uh-ohs and peeked in...The uh-ohs were all still in there safe-safe...

uh oh

uh oh

The uh-oh heart
Let Them out Like
old·old friends...

but They floated
away... Like...
nothing...

Uh-oh, it thought,

maybe there's no such thing as safe-safe.

Although The uh-oh hearT feLT aLL aLone, The sky was righT There holding iT wiTh iTs wide-wide openness.

And the future Took Strange shape-shape
you've got to be kidding me

Hope found its own
open -

opening

and The uh-oh hearT
grew
(in spiTe of itseLf)

ThankfuL-ThankfuL
for momenTs Like This.

And although the uh-oh
heart was not very good at
math-math, it saw that
these moments added up
to something...

Little by Little... Bit by Bit... It Lifted

and grew stronger

It waved

in the wind-
wind of change.

All that the other heart had taught the uh-oh heart about Life and its La-La's began to come back... as if they had never left, as if they were just inside- inside all the time...

The uh-oh hearT was full-full of sad and happy all mixy-mixed. It was alive-alive!

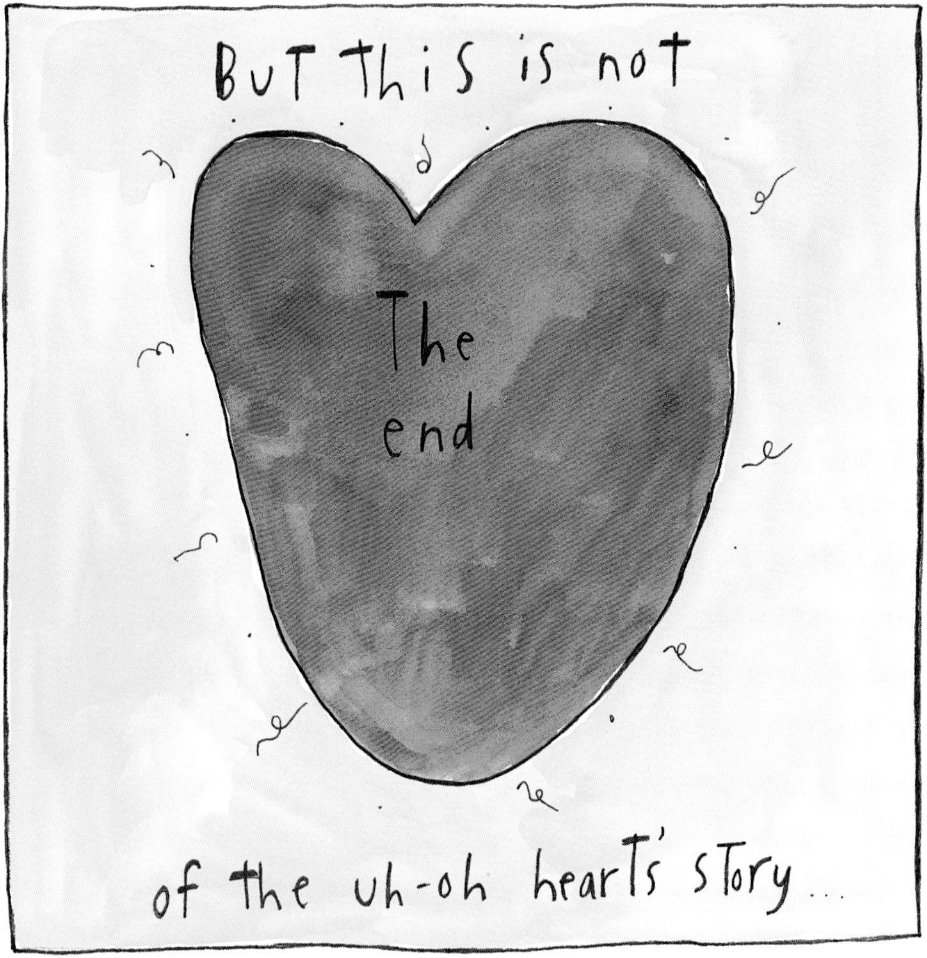
But this is not
The end
of the uh-oh hearts' story...

The uh-oh hearT's sTory goes on-on. Because The uh-oh hearT, withouT iTs uh-ohs, (alThough iT kepT a few as all hearTs do) began To grow...

and grow

and grow

uNTiL iT overfLowed

and The World became
more - more Than iT was...

and
full-
full

of the opposite of fear
or, as some people call it,
Love ...
hu ho?
yes
sniff sniff

the poinT-poinT

About the Author

Sandy Gingras is an artist and writer with her own design company called "How To Live" (visit her website at www.how-to-live.com). She and her son, three cats and a fat yellow Labrador live next to a salt marsh on Long Beach Island, New Jersey, where she is active in efforts to preserve open space and wetlands.

If you liked this book, you may also enjoy these other books by Sandy Gingras:

How To be a Friend
ISBN 0-945582-99-4
$12.95 hardcover

A little book that celebrates friendship.

How To Live at the Beach
ISBN 0-945582-73-0
$12.95 hardcover

"Like the ocean itself, this book nourishes the mind, heart, and soul."
— Coastal Living Magazine

How To Live on an Island
ISBN 0-945582-57-9
$11.95 hardcover

"...there's no truer place than an island."

Reasons to be Happy at the Beach
ISBN 0-945582-98-6
$16.95 hardcover

"Happiness is...all around us. We are looking at it, breathing it, holding it in our hands."

Down The Shore Publishing offers other book and calendar titles (with a special emphasis on the mid-Atlantic coast). For a free catalog, or to be added to our mailing list, just send us a request:

Down The Shore Publishing
P.O. Box 3100
Harvey Cedars, NJ 08008

www.down-the-shore.com

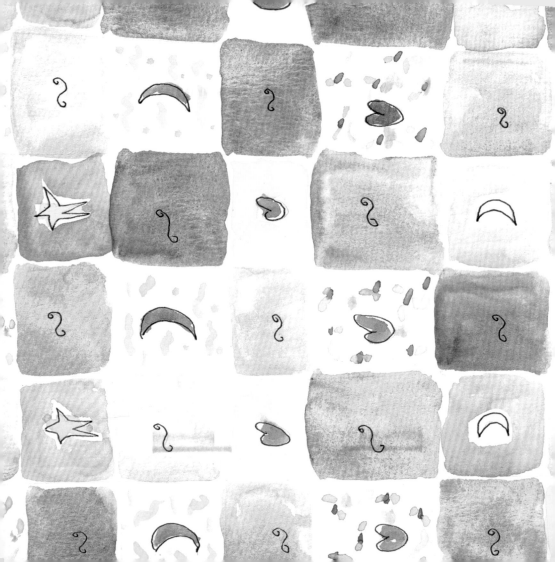